How Do Animals use...
Their Mouths?

Lynn Stone

Rourke
Publishing LLC
Vero Beach, Florida 32964

www.rourkepublishing.com

PHOTO CREDITS: All Photos © Lynn Stone, except pg. 19 © Bruse Coleman

Editor: Robert Stengard-Olliges

Cover design by: Nicola Stratford, bdpublishing.com

Library of Congress Cataloging-in-Publication Data

Stone, Lynn M.
  How do animals use their mouths? / Lynn Stone.
     p. cm. -- (How do aniamls use--?)
  ISBN 978-1-60044-506-4
  1. Mouth--Juvenile literature. I. Title.
  QL857.S76 2008
  591.4'4--dc22
                                2007015169

Printed in the USA

CG/CG

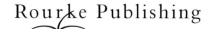

Rourke Publishing

www.rourkepublishing.com – rourke@rourkepublishing.com
Post Office Box 3328, Vero Beach, FL 32964

Animals use their mouths for many things.

A **bear** uses its mouth to catch a fish.

A panda uses its mouth to eat bamboo.

A **snake** uses its mouth to eat a rat.

A **caterpillar** uses its mouth to eat a leaf.

A tiger uses its mouth to drink water.

Seals use their mouths to fight.

A **pelican** uses its mouth to feed its chick.

A lion uses its mouth to carry
its cub.

Animal mouths can do
many things.

Glossary

bear (bair) – a large animal with fur, sharp claws and teeth

caterpillar (KAT urh pil uhr) – a short, furry worm with tiny legs

pelican (PEL uh kuhn) – a big bird that lives by the sea

seal (seel) – a mammal that lives in the ocean and on land

snake (snayk) – a long, thin reptile that has no legs

Index

Further Reading

Souza, Dun. *Look What Mouths Can Do*. Lerner Classroom, 2007.

Perkins, Wendy. *Let's Look at Animal Teeth*. Pebble Press, 2007.

Websites

www.kidsites.com/sites-edu/animals.htm

animal.discovery.com

About the Author

Lynn M. Stone is the author of more than 400 children's books. He is a talented natural history photographer as well. Lynn, a former teacher, travels worldwide to photograph wildlife in its natural habitat.